AF273539

Preface

Determination of the size of a sphere is quite easy: You can describe it solely from the radius, i.e. you only need one single value. However, when it comes to particles in pharmaceutical products, determination of sizes are often much more complex than assumed – and as particle size is one of the most important single factors for product behaviour, it is a scientific area of vast interest.

At Particle Analytical, we have been working with determination of particle sizes for the pharmaceutical industry since 2000. Our customers have in general showed a large interest for an introduction to this area from a down-to-earth and practical perspective. The intended readers of this booklet are pharmacists and technicians working with determination of particles sizes. This booklet is not meant as a thorough introduction into theory behind determination of particle sizes, and only a limited number of references will be given: The booklet is primarily based on our own experiences and is a practical introduction to the area with a brief introduction to "why" and "how" in determination of particle sizes.

Particle Analytical is a cGMP compliant company dedicated to supporting customers within the field of particle analysis/powder analysis. Particle Analytical support R&D, production and quality assurance. www.particle.dk

Determination of particle sizes

How?

© 2014 Karin Liltorp, Søren Lund Kristensen, Thomas Andresen
Forlag: BoD – København, Danmark
Fremstilling: BoD – Norderstedt, Tyskland

ISBN 978-87-7145-657-8

Table of content

Introduction

By far the most important physical property of particulate samples in pharmaceutical development is particle size. Particle size determination is routinely carried out across a wide range of industries and is often a critical parameter in the manufacture of pharmaceutical products. Particle size has a direct influence on material properties such as:

- Bioavailability for oral drugs
- Stability in suspension – e.g. sedimentation
- Efficacy of delivery – e.g. asthma inhalers
- Appearance – e.g. powder coatings
- Flowability and handling – e.g. granules
- Packing density and porosity

Thus, particle size is of immense importance for all solid pharmaceutical products, both in relation to processability and bioavailability. Particle size during production is not always easily controlled: Even slight changes in manufacturing conditions might lead to quite large size or morphology changes and these changes might be critical for the current product (blending properties, dissolution rate, agglomeration tendencies, etc.) According to regulatory authorities (ICH guidelines), particle size distribution should be known – and controlled. Ultimately, this is carried out to protect the patients, but also to avoid unpleasant surprises during manufacturing.

Measurement of particle size is not, unlike many other analytical techniques, an exact technique and a true value of the size does not exist. A range of analytical techniques is available for determination of particle size; these all have their strengths and weaknesses. As a consequence of the complexity of particle size and shape, the major part of particle-sizing techniques are restricted to "assuming" that the material being measured is spherical and the particle size is reported as the diameter of the "equivalent sphere" which would give the same response as the particle being measured.

So what is the <u>right</u> particle size? Imagine a needle shaped particle: It is obvious that the measured size of such a particle will vary quite significantly if you analyse it by microscopy (where you will get the maximum length) or sieving analysis (where you might get the minimum thickness)! Thus, the size reported for a particle will be very dependent on the physical property measured by the chosen technique - and you cannot argue that one of these methods is more correct than the other. Thus, one should always be aware how the particle sizes are measured – and that results from different techniques cannot be expected to give the same result.

A golden standard method for determination of particle sizes is laser diffraction. This method has unique strengths: It allows measurement of a large number of particle and is very robust. However, a laser diffraction method requires thorough validation - including correlation to other techniques, such as microscopy. This booklet describes the different methods used in determination of particle sizes - with primary focus on laser diffraction. Further, the booklet highlights the pitfalls that should be avoided when measuring particle sizes.

What is the size of a needle?
It definitely depends on how you chose to measure it: Would you like to know the length or the thickness? How will you measure it? Using a ruler or a sliding gauge? This is simple illustration of one of the challenges in determination of particle sizes.

What is a particle?

- From Wikipedia: "A particle is a small localized object to which can be ascribed several physical properties such as volume or mass."
- In relation to a pharmaceutical drug, particle relates to a *network* of drug molecules bound to each other in a more or less structured manner – forming solid "clusters" (particles) .
- The individual molecules in a particle are held together by hydrogen bonding, Van der Wall - or ionic forces, either in an amorphous assembly (unordered) or in a crystalline structure (ordered).
- *Tablets* and *capsules* used for pharmaceutical products are "made of" particles of various particle sizes.
- The nature and size of the particles determines the *physical properties* of the drug with regard to stability, solubility, dissolution, reactivity etc.

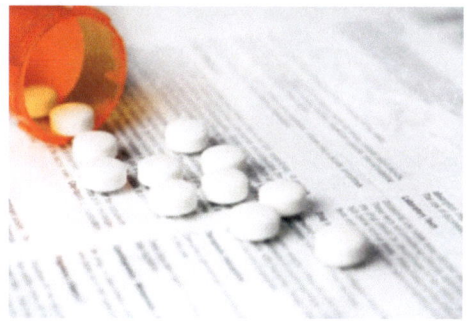

Why we care about particle sizes

Particle size is essential in order to understand and control drugs during development. Lack of control of particle sizes might have large consequences for the behaviour of the compound during manufacturing and -ultimately- *in vivo*. Overall, the particle size might be critical in relation to patient safety with regard to:

1. **Content in final product**: Does the product contain the desired amount of API? Inhomogeneous distribution of the API in the final product due to change in "mixing properties" might be a direct consequence of changes in particle size and morphology.
2. **Stability**: Is the product stable? A change in particle size or crystal form might affect the interactions of the API with the excipients or surrounding water, i.e. "closer contact" and larger assessable surface for smaller particles could lead to increased reactivity.
3. **Dissolution rate**: Is the API released at a "controlled rate" *in vivo*? Change in particle size gives higher/lower dissolution rate and thereby bioavailability.

Particle size and bioavailability

A molecule in a particle is not directly "bioavailable", as the particles will not be absorbed in the body. Only the dissolved form of a compound will be absorbed in the human body.

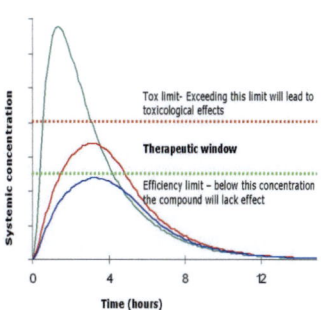

Thus, as long as the compound exists in particles, it is unavailable for the blood stream, and will not reach the "site of action". Dissolution of particles in a tablet will begin in the stomach. Depending on the particle size and the solubility of the compound, part of the total dose is dissolved here. Following, the compound enters duodenum and continues into jejunum, where absorption will take place. Depending on the initial dissolution rate, part of the dose will be available for absorption.

Large particles will dissolve more slowly than small particles. The plasma profile of a virtual patient is shown: To obtain the desired effect of a drug, a certain plasma profile should be reached – here illustrated by the red curve. Too low exposure (for instance caused by too large particles) could lead to lack of effect (blue curve) – and too high exposure (caused by too small particles) would lead to toxicological effects (green curve).

Why determination of sizes is not straight forward

For a perfect sphere it is quite easy to determine the particle size: You only need the diameter. If all particles were spherical it would be quite easy to determine the particle size using the available methods. Unfortunately molecular systems very seldom form nice spherical particles. Instead they form various other shapes – and all particles in a mixture have different particle size. Below you see a Scanning Electron Microscopy (SEM) picture of a pharmaceutical compound. If you were to describe the particle sizes in this mixture – how would you do it?

Would you describe all particles separately? Probably not, as it will be quite time consuming! Would you report the length (which length?), the height (which height?) – or the relation between these? From looking at the picture above it is quite clear that it is not a simple task to describe the particle size/particle size distribution as particles of various sizes and shapes are present.

Analysing particle sizes is not like performing an ID test: You cannot "just" put the sample in the instrument – and out comes "the answer". Before you perform a particle size analysis you should be very careful about what method you use – and be aware of the strengths and weaknesses of the various methods: There is not such a thing as a perfect description of particle sizes, but a combination of methods can give you a reliable description in order to control your product. In the following sections some of the methods used for determination of particle size are summarized – including strengths and weaknesses.

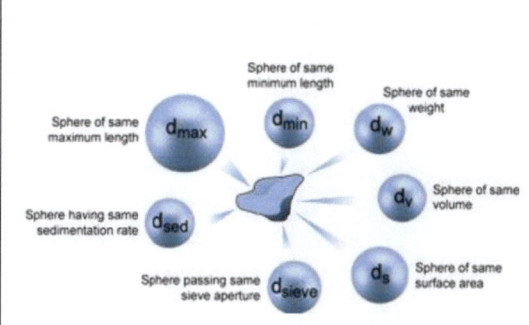

As shown in the figure you can chose between various diameters in describing the particles in a sample – and not one of these diameters are the "correct" diameter.

Again: using the needle shaped particle as an extreme: Huge variation between the determined sizes might exist. How would you prefer the diameter of the particles reported? Many opportunities exist – and not one diameter is more correct than another.

Primary particles versus agglomerates/aggregates

In determination of particle sizes it is important to distinguish between primary particles and agglomerates/aggregates. Using SEM it is easily seen whether the particles have tendencies to aggregate – and if the sizes measured by laser diffraction reflect the primary particles or the aggregates.

The presence of aggregates might in some cases have a large impact on product behaviour – and in other cases these aggregates might be dispersed into primary particles by gentle mechanical treatment and therefore the effect on overall product behaviour is limited.

SEM is the optimal method for distinguishing between primary particles and aggregates as all details are seen.

From this picture, it is possible to estimate the sizes of the primary particles and further to evaluate the degree of aggregation. This information is generally used for verifying an indirect measurement of particle sizes such as laser diffraction.

Particle morphology

Not only are the sizes of the particles relevant for the particle behaviour: The morphology has a large impact, as slight changes in, for instance, surface might affect the properties during processing. Information about the morphology of the particles is obtained from optical microscopy and SEM. European Pharmacopoeia (2.9.37) uses following descriptions in relation to of particle morphology:

Particle shape characterisation.
For irregularly shaped particles, characterisation of particle size must also include information on particle shape. The homogeneity of the powder must be checked using appropriate magnification. The following defines some commonly used descriptors of particle shape (see Figure).
— *acicular*: slender, needle-like particle of similar width and thickness,
— *columnar*: long, thin particle with a width and thickness that are greater than those of an acicular particle,
— *flake*: thin, flat particle of similar length and width,
— *plate*: flat particle of similar length and width but with greater thickness than a flake particle,
— *lath*: long, thin, blade-like particle,
— *equant*: particle of similar length, width, and thickness; both cubical and spherical particles are included.

General observations.
A particle is generally considered to be the smallest discrete unit. A particle may be a liquid or semi-solid droplet; a single crystal or polycrystalline; amorphous or an agglomerate. Particles may be associated. This degree of association may be described by the following terms:
— *lamellar*: stacked plates,
— *aggregate*: mass of adhered particles,
— *agglomerate*: fused or cemented particles,
— *conglomerate*: mixture of 2 or more types of particles,
— *spherulite*: radial cluster,
— *drusy*: particle covered with tiny particles.

Particle condition may be described by the following terms:
– *edges*: angular, rounded, smooth, sharp, fractured,
– *optical*: color (using proper color balancing filters), transparent, translucent, opaque,
– *defects*: occlusions, inclusions.

Surface characteristics may be described as:
– *cracked*: partial split, break, or fissure,
– *smooth*: free of irregularities, roughness, or projections,
– *porous*: having openings or passageways,
– *rough*: bumpy, uneven, not smooth,
– *pitted*: small indentations.

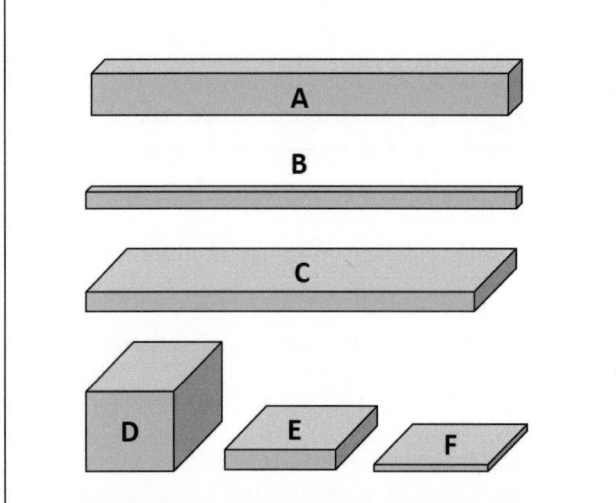

A. Columnar
B. Acicular
C. Lath
D. Equant
E. Plate
F: Flake

Based on European Pharmacopoeia (2.9.37), the particles can be described from the above shapes. In practice, these shapes are seldom very similar to the shapes of real particles. It implies that the description of particle morphology is very subjective (e.g., is it "plates" or "flakes" – or rather "laths") Thus, a description of the particles should preferably be combined with a SEM picture of the particles.

Regulatory requirements

In the ICH guidelines several references to determination of particle sizes are found (e.g. ICH Q6A, Q8 and Q9). – including the decision tree shown here. According to the decision tree, particle specification should be set if the particle size is critical to either dissolution, processability, stability, content uniformity or product appearance – which in practice mean "always" – and this goes for the API as well as the excipients. The requirement for setting specification further implies that a validated method is needed.

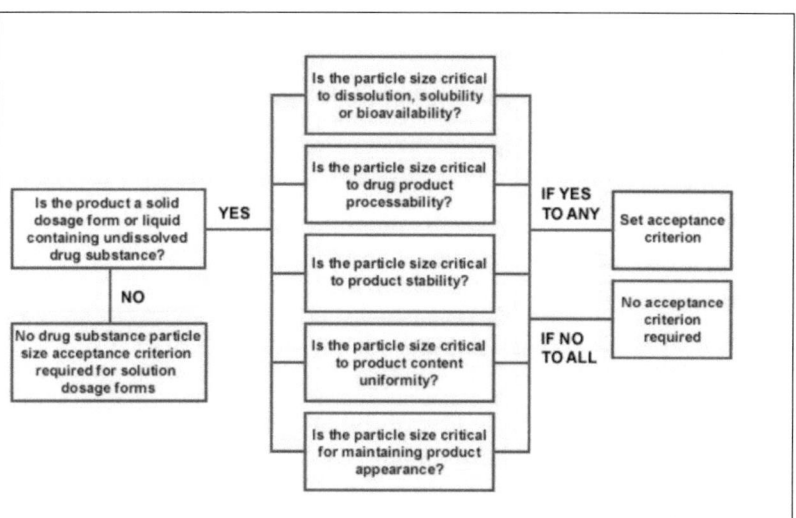

From ICH Q6A: A decision tree describing the potential need for setting particle specifications. Only in theory it is possible to answer "no" to all, thus in practice acceptance criteria for particle sizes always have to be set.

Setting particle specifications

The main concern in relation to the regulatory requirements is to secure that the drug is "predictable" with respect to particle properties when given to a patient. When setting the particle specification it should be based on a critical evaluation of the potential risks – and the specifications should not be set too narrow unless it actually poses a potential risk to the patient. Thus, risk assessment should include the effect of particle size, including evaluation of a minimum and maximum size.

Risk Assessment

1. What are **the risks** in relation to changes in particle sizes? The risk is that the particles in the product change size and morphology leading to changes in dissolution profile etc.
2. The **probability** of changes in particle size depends on how easy it is to control sizes during manufacturing. This is very dependent on the specific product and the robustness of the manufacturing process.
3. What are the **consequences** if it happens? If the particles in the product change, the consequences are highly dependent on the *therapeutic window* of the drug and whether or not the particle size need to be very well controlled in order to obtain the right therapeutic effect.

Patient safety and particle sizes

1. *A change in particle size changes the dissolution profile: Larger particles might lead to lower bioavailability*
2. *Too small particle sizes in inhalation products might be dangerous!*

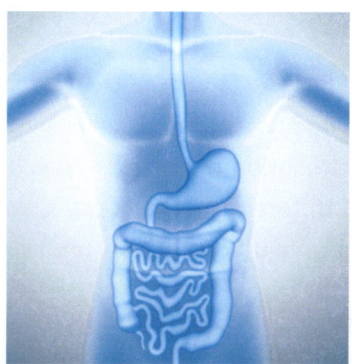

3. *A change in particle size or morphology might affect the mixing properties during manufacturing leading to inhomogeneous distribution.*
4. *A change in particle size/morphology might affect stability, e.g. the interactions of the API with the excipients and could lead to unwanted reactions and/or degradation of the API.*

Thus, the particle specifications should be based on scientifically well-founded rationales. You do not want to set the limits too narrow as it reduces freedom during manufacturing. On the other hand, you want to be sure that the changes in particles properties do not affect the patient safety.

To evaluate the effect of particle size one should, in the ideal world, produce particles of various sizes and analyse these with regard to all relevant properties. However, this is usually not possible, as controlling particle sizes during manufacturing is not straight forward – and the experimental work might be quite tedious. Instead, a combination of experiments and calculations (with regard to dissolution and blending) could be used.

Methods in determination of particle sizes

As already mentioned, several methods are available for determination of particle sizes. In order to verify the measured sizes, different methods are always required. Some of the most commonly used methods are listed below.

Instrument	How	Comments
Laser diffraction	Particles are dispersed in air or a dispersion media – and exposed to a laser beam. The scattered light is translated into a particle size distribution.	A robust method for obtaining a full overview of the particle sizes, as a large number of particles are analysed. However, a validated method is needed in order to secure that the laser diffraction results actually describes the product- and to secure that the particles are not altered during sample preparation..
Optical Microscopy	Particles are dispersed on a glass slide and sizes are determined using an appropriate magnification.	Easy method to get a fast view of the particle sizes – and information about shape. A very useful method in verification of laser diffraction results. It is not always possible to distinguish primary particles and agglomerates. Very difficult/time consuming to get a statistically full description of the particle sizes. Results usually operator dependent.
Scanning Electron Microscopy (SEM)	A scanning electron microscope produces images of a sample by scanning it with a focused beam of electrons.	A unique method in studying the primary particles. Same advantages as from microscopy with regard to particle size – including 3D information. Detailed information about morphology and primary particles but only on a very limited amount of material.

BET	The BET instrument determines the specific surface area: The volume of gas adsorbed to the surface of the particles is measured at the boiling point of nitrogen. The amount of adsorbed gas is correlated to the total surface area of the particles including pores in the surface.	The surface area is not directly correlated to the particle sizes. However, the particle size is reflected in the surface area, as smaller particles have a larger surface area. The method is especially useful to investigate differences between particles of "same size" – i.e. sometimes, the surface area might differ, leading to very different properties with regard to dissolution. The method is very well suited for porous or lamellar materials, as you hereby obtain information about structure.
Sieving analysis	The fraction of particles passing through different sieve sizes is determined.	Equipment is very cheap and useful if you want to search for single large particles in your mixture. Requires a large sample amount and is quite time consuming. Very limited information about "fines" can be derived.

Laser diffraction

By laser diffraction analysis it is possible to measure particles size distribution for particles in the size region between <1 μm to around 3 mm for a very large number of particles. Various different equipment exist (e.g. Malvern and Sympatec). For all laser diffraction instruments, the overall principle is to disperse the powder sample in either air or a suitable liquid media and expose it to a laser beam. The diffracted light is detected and translated into a particle size distribution. It should be highlighted that the results from different equipment cannot be directly compared, as variations in the measurement principles will lead to different results.

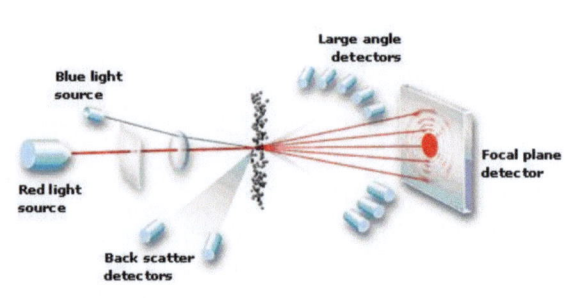

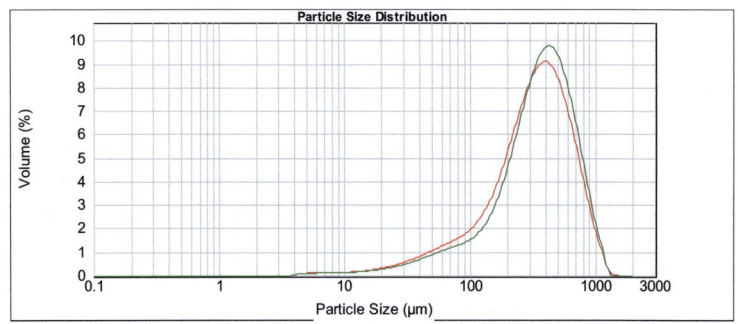

A laser diffraction instrument has a flow-through cell for dispersion of particles in liquid media or a dry dispenser for dispersion of particles in air. Wet dispersion presupposes that the particles are insoluble in the liquid. The laser passes through the dispersion media and is diffracted by the particles. It is ensured that the particles pass the laser beam in a homogeneous stream by securing a uniform dispersion of the sample in the chosen media. The diffraction pattern is measured by detectors, and the signal is then transformed to a particle size distribution based on an optical model: The pattern is characteristic of the particle size and using mathematical analysis the result is transformed into an accurate, repeatable picture of the size distribution.

Laser diffraction is known to be a very robust method – but some dangerous pitfall exist: By laser diffraction you do not obtain a direct measurement of the particles: The signals from the measurement is "translated" into a particle size by different calculation methods, assuming that the particles are spherical which might be far from true.

Further, the particles are mechanically affected during measurement: The particles will be exposed to pressure, stirring etc. – thus during validation, it should be very carefully studied that this mechanical treatment does not alter the particles. This subject will be discussed in more detail under the section about method validation.

Models for determination of particle size distribution

The translation of the laser scattering pattern is based on either *Fraunhofer* or *Mie* theory. In the Fraunhofer model it is assumed that the particles interacting with the laser beam are spherical and that the laser light does not "enter" the particles (i.e. the particles are not transparent) – both assumptions are not true, but in in most cases the model has shown to give valid results. The Mie theory also assumes spherical particles, but further it is taken into account that the particles are transparent and absorbs part of the light. Thus, this model is theoretically more correct. However, the use of Mie theory presupposes knowledge of the refractive index of the particles and the dispersion media, and if these parameters are not known, the results might lead to serious misinterpretation.

If you are not using the right calculation method and correct parameters, this might lead to large over- or underestimation –

especially of the presence of small particles! The consequence might be severe – as for instance a too high or too low exposure in vivo. It is generally agreed that the use of Fraunhofer is suitable for large particles, but in the small-particle-end the Mie theory provides the greatest accuracy. However, the refractive index <u>must</u> be known. Thus, if the real and imaginary parts of the refractive index are not known, the Fraunhofer model should always be used. The refractive index is determined experimentally.

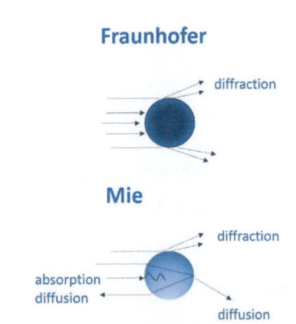

Fraunhofer

diffraction

Mie

diffraction

absorption
diffusion

diffusion

Translating diffraction pattern into particle size
The Fraunhofer model assumes that the particles interacting with the laser beam are spherical and that the laser light does not "enter" the particles.

(i.e. the particles are not transparent) The Mie theory also assumes spherical particles, but further it is taken into account that the particles are transparent and absorbs part of the light.

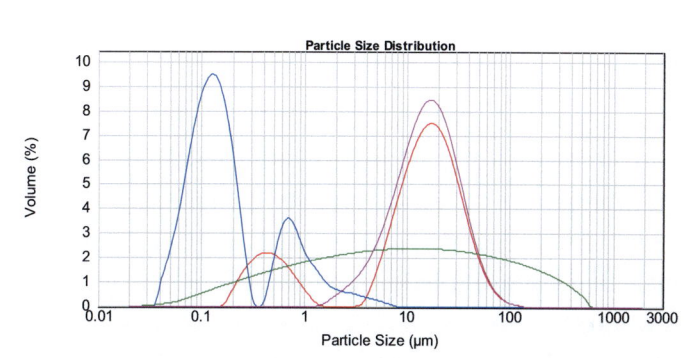

Particle Size Distribution

It is very important to use the correct refractive index when applying the Mie model for calculation of particle sizes! The figure shows the result from a laser diffraction measurement: All curves are from the same measurement and the only difference is that the refractive index of the particles has been set to values between 1.3 and 1.6 (i.e. values that are "normal" for organic material). As shown, the results vary significantly. Thus, If the refractive index of the particles is not known, the Mie model should not be used!

Optical Microscopy and digital image analysis

Using optical microscopy is very relevant for verifying the results from laser diffraction: By magnifying the particles, it is possible to evaluate the sizes and see the overall morphology (i.e. needles, plates or "spheres"). Microscopy and digital image analysis can be used for magnification up to *1000 and is used for:

- Determination of particle size distribution, where the size of a specified number of particles are determined. For size distribution purposes more than 3000 particles are typically processed and the sizes in such a determination can be compared to laser diffraction results.
- More detailed information about particle characteristics, for instance particle shape and aspect ratio (ratio between breadth and length). These parameters cannot be examined by laser diffraction, and might be relevant in understanding product behaviour.

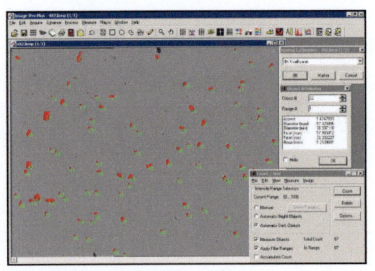

A challenge in using optical microscopy is to find the right threshold: What are particles and what is "background noise". Using digital image analysis the sizes of the particles is determined automatically from this threshold.

It should be noted that optical microscopy is not always ideal for distinguishing between aggregates and primary particles – and in many cases, SEM is required as an additional analysis.

Optical microscopy is very often used for verification of the results obtained by laser diffraction. In general it is expected that the results from the two measurements is more or less in the same region. However, often it is observed that one curve I shifted relative to the other. It might be due to special particle characteristics (e.g. needle shaped particles) or due to the fact that the statistical accuracy of a microscopy measurement is much

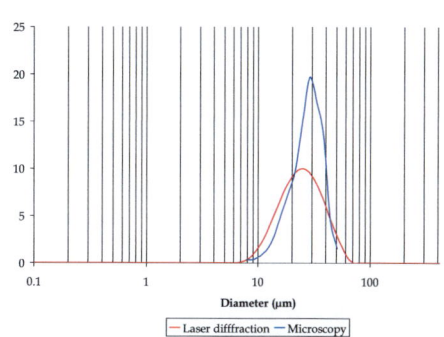

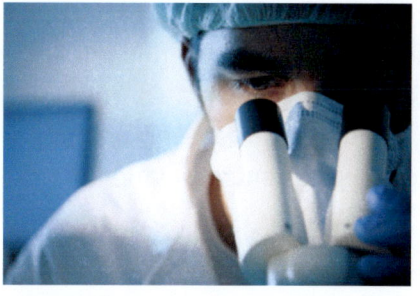

lower as relatively few particles are examined. In the current example the correlation between the measurements is quite good.

SEM

A scanning electron microscope (SEM) produces images of a sample by scanning it with a focused beam of electrons. Detectors collect backscattered electrons from the sample surface and the signals are converted into a picture of the particles.

The large advantage of SEM in relation to ordinary light microscopy is that the particles can be studies in detail: SEM allows a much higher magnification (>100,000X) and greater depth of focus up to 100 times that of light microscopy. It is a unique method in differing primary particles from aggregates/agglomerates. Thus, SEM is used in visualisation of crystal shape, surface morphology and structure of particles or agglomerates and evaluation of product surface characteristics.

For conventional imaging in the SEM, specimens must be electrically conductive, at least at the surface, and electrically grounded to prevent the accumulation of electrostatic charge at the surface. Nonconductive specimens such as pharmaceutical products are therefore usually coated with an ultrathin coating of electrically conducting material, deposited on the sample by low-vacuum sputter coating.

A SEM picture of a pharmaceutical material. It is observed that the major part of the particles are needles (acicular and of various thickness), but also more "cubic" (equant) particles are seen. The tendency to aggregate is very limited for this material.

This pharmaceutical material forms plates rather than needles. Some tendency to aggregate is observed: The smaller particles seem to adhere to the larger particles.

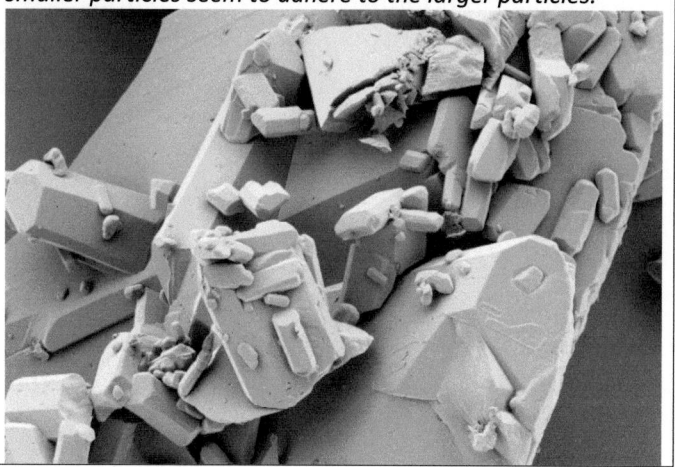

BET

By BET (method named after Brunauer, Emmett and Teller) the *specific surface area* of a sample is measured. The surface area of a sample is not directly correlated to the particle sizes. However, the particle size is reflected in the surface area, as smaller particles have a larger surface area. The method is especially useful to investigate differences between particles of apparently "same size" as measured by laser diffraction.

In some case the surface area might differ significantly, leading to very different properties with regard to dissolution – as would be the case for the mushroom shown below: In a laser measurement only the outer size will be reflected, whereas BET would give further information about lamellar structure.

Thus, the method is very well suited for porous or lamellar materials, as you hereby obtain information about structure. This information is used to predict the dissolution rate, as this rate is proportional to the specific surface area. Thus, the surface area can be used to predict bioavailability. Further, it is useful in evaluation of product performance and manufacturing consistency. BET might give additional interesting information about materials in cases the particle size by laser diffraction does not fully describe the particle properties.

In a BET measurement, the samples are dried with nitrogen purging, or in a vacuum applying elevated temperatures. The specific surface area of a powder is determined by physical adsorption of a gas (traditionally nitrogen is used) on the surface of the solid and by calculating the amount of adsorbate gas corresponding to a monomolecular layer on the surface. This physical adsorption results from relatively weak forces (van der Waals forces) between the adsorbate gas molecules and the adsorbent surface area of the test powder. The amount of adsorbed gas is correlated to the total surface area of the particles including pores in the surface. The determination is usually carried out at the boiling temperature of liquid nitrogen.

In a BET measurement the amount of nitrogen absorbed to the surface of the material is determined – and this amount is translated into a total surface area.

Before the specific surface area of the sample can be determined, it is necessary to remove gases and vapour that may have become physically adsorbed onto the surface after manufacture and during treatment, handling and storage. If outgassing is not achieved, the specific surface area may be reduced or may be variable because an intermediate area of the surface is covered with molecules of the previously adsorbed gases or vapour.

Method validation in laser diffraction

As already mentioned measurement of particle size is not an exact technique and therefore does not express a "true" value. This is a major difference to other quantitative measurements as by HPLC, GC etc. Laser diffraction is the golden standard method for determination of particle sizes in the pharmaceutical industry why the focus on the following section is on validation of such a diffraction method – using the other experimental methods in verification of the results. According to the ICH guideline, the parameters listed in the table should be examined in relation to validation of analytical methods – however, not all of these apply for determination of particle sizes by laser diffraction.

Parameter	Comment
Accuracy	A laser diffraction method is, per definition, not accurate. However, comparison of results from a laser diffraction measurement with other methods might replace accuracy.
Precision	Applies.
Specificity	Particle size is not specific. Not applicable.
Detection Limit	It is not possible to define a detection limit – in theory, the size of one particle can be determined. Not applicable.
Quantification Limit	It is not possible to define a detection limit – in theory, the size of one particle can be determined. Not applicable.
Linearity	Determination of sizes does not depend on concentration of particles. However, the maximum concentration should be determined in a robustness test. Not applicable.
Range	Does an upper or lower size limit exist for the current method? It might also be part of the robustness testing.
Robustness	*Very* important in relation to determination of particle sizes. The need for robustness testing is highlighted in the FDA guidance

According to USP: "It is the responsibility of the user to demonstrate the applicability of the instrument for its intended use and to validate any method prior to its adoption for routine use." A validation of method of analysis should include:

- Validation protocol including setting acceptance criteria
- Verification of sample stability
- Verification of the repeatability of the method
- Robustness (including intermediate precision)
- Critical batches
- Correlation to SEM of all batches
- Correlation to microscopy of all batches
- Validation report including all documentation

Test	Comments
Finding a suitable dispersion medium	Should air or liquid be used? It depends on the particle characteristics as explained in more detail in following section.
Test of sample stability in the medium	It should be ensured that dissolution or alteration of the particles does not take place during measurement. This also includes test of e.g. stirring and sonication in the current media.
Test of repeatability of the method	A number of measurements on the same sample should secure that it is possible to obtain the same result each time
SEM	For correlation: SEM is used to verify that the measured particles sizes reflect the actual particle sizes –and to verify the size interval.

Particle size distribution by microscopy	Determining particle sizes for a number of particles (e.g. 3000) for correlation to laser diffraction.
Test of other batches	If different qualities of the same product exists (e.g. different suppliers, micronized versus non-micronized, etc.), it is wise to test if the method is suitable for all types.

Wet or dry dispersion

For free flowing and large particle, dry dispersion might be best suited, whereas wet dispersion might be preferred for smaller particles. Dry dispersion requires much more sample than wet dispersion (> 2 g) whereas valid results for a wet dispersion method requires much less (< 0.5 or less). One of the differences between dry and wet dispersion is how the particles are exposed to the laser beam: In wet dispersion the sample is circulated in the system in a liquid, i.e. you can chose any measuring time, as long as the particles are not affected by the stirring. In dry dispersion, the measurement time is limited, as the powder is only in the air stream for a short period while it passes the laser beam.

In general, one cannot argue that one of these methods is more correct than the other: In both cases, the samples are exposed to different mechanical stress that might alter the material so selection of the "best method" depends on the material in question. Depending on whether a dry or wet dispersion method has been chosen, different parameters should be further examined:

Wet dispersion
Suitability of dispersion media
Stirring speed
Obscuration interval
Measurement time
Sonication test (if necessary)
Surfactant concentration (if necessary)

Number of required determinations to minimize the uncertainty of the result & Number of required measurements per determination to ensure a representative part of the sample is measured.

Dry dispersion
Pressure determination
Obscuration interval
Feed rate
Sample amount
Slit opening
Sieve (if necessary) and number of dispersion balls (if necessary)
Number of required determinations to minimize the uncertainty of the results.

Sampling

A laser measurement is generally very robust. However, it is essential that the measured sample is representative for the material and this is very dependent on the sampling procedure. Sampling is a science of its own and will not be treated in this booklet.

Finding the right dispersion media

A good dispersion media requires that the particles does not dissolve. Initial experiment can be performed by adding the material to a number of solvents and visually observe if it dissolves. When these initial experiments indicates that dissolution does not take place, it should be further examined on the laser instrument: Dissolution can be examined directly from a measurement, as it will be observed as a change in particle size distribution and a continuously lowering of the obscuration. Water is the obvious first choice as dispersion medium – thus if the product does not dissolve in water this should be the media: It makes cleaning of the instrument much easier. In some cases where the product does not dissolve in water, but do not disperse properly, a surfactant could be added. When addition of a surfactant is necessary to obtain a homogenous dispersion of the particles, the chosen amount should be as low as possible while still securing proper dispersion. If water is not suitable for the material, any other liquid can be chosen, but coloured media should be avoided, as these will absorb light. If you have a product with high density, it might be preferred to use a dispersion media with high density too in order to prevent sedimentation.

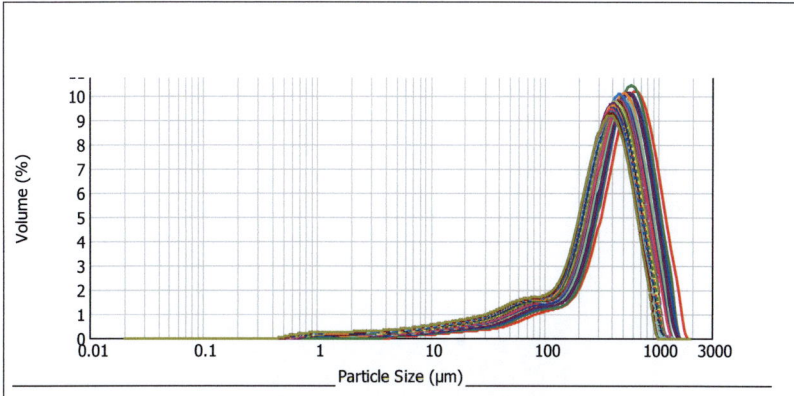

Finding the right dispersion media

A stability test should be performed in the chosen media: If dissolution takes place during the first couple of minutes it will usually be observed as a shift towards larger particles sizes (i.e. the smaller particles dissolve). If a shift from larger to smaller particles are observed it might be due to sedimentation of large particles. The above curve represent such a stability, and as observed a change in the peak maximum occur.

Cleaning

Cleaning between measurements can be quite time consuming! In general a solvent that dissolves the material should be used (i.e. the dispersion media is not suited for the following cleaning). Further, it is required that the chosen cleaning liquid is miscible with the dispersion media.

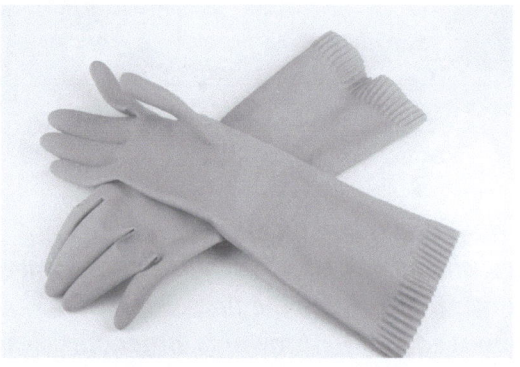

Background

The right signal to noise ration should be known in order to obtain reliable results. Some noise cannot be avoided – especially at the detectors close to the laser beam. This noise is arising from dust in the surrounding air. The background measurement is highest on detector 1 and decreasing with the higher detector numbers. If peaks are observed at the higher detector numbers, it indicates that particles are observed in the system. It might be either particles from the last measurement or air bubbles. The level of acceptable noise should be set based on the chosen dispersion media, as some differences in the level will be observed.

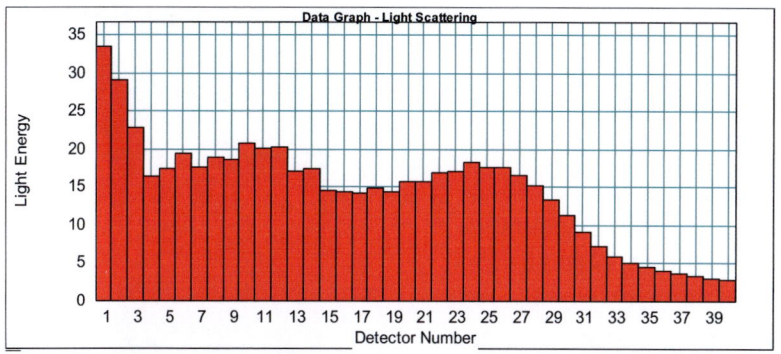

Pollution of the system will be seen most clearly at the higher detector numbers. In this case the system is not fully clean as seen as an increasing intensity around detector 25, but the level of noise is, for most purposes, acceptable.

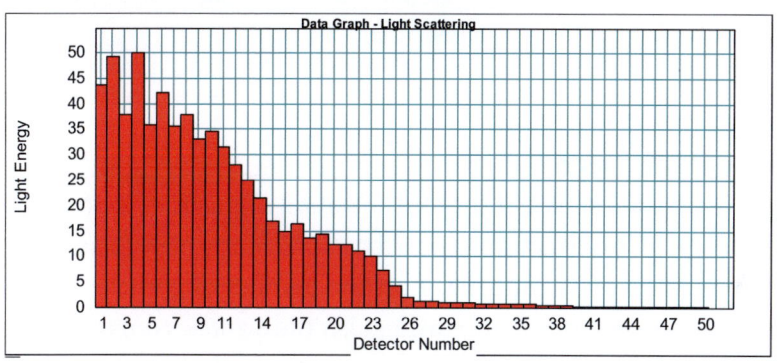

The background signals observed above is what can generally be expected for a measurement: A decrease in signals when going from the low-number detectors to the larger numbers.

Stirring speed

Stirring is necessary in order to obtain a homogenous dispersion when using wet dispersion: Without stirring the particle might sediment. Thus, stirring should ensure that all particles are observed during measurement, i.e. the large particles should be dispersed.

Too high might lead to air bubbles in the dispersion media – especially if a surfactant is added. Further, too high stirring speed might alter the particles.

Obscuration interval

The obscuration is the optical concentration of particles in the laser beam. This obscuration should be sufficiently high to assure a valid signal to noise ratio, i.e. a certain number of particles should be present in order to distinguish the signals from noise (dust etc.). However, if the obscuration is too high there is a risk of multiple scattering and this will lead to wrong interpretation of results: Multiple scattering occurs when there is an "overlap" of particles in the laser beam. In this case the scattered light will not reflect the actual particle sizes. Thus, during method development this upper limit should be set. Multiple scattering might be observed as "extra" peaks on the results when a certain obscuration level is reached.

Sonication

When sonication is applied to a sample, the particles will be affected! In general, sonication is a harsh treatment, and care should be taken to avoid alteration of the particles. It should further be taken into account that the energy applied during sonication depends on the sonication equipment, and care should be taken using the same "energy level" each time.

In general: When you are using sonication there is a large risk that you are not getting the right particle sizes but are actually determining the sizes of the broken particles. However, in some cases sonication might be the best methods to separate the aggregates. Thus, the effect of sonication should always be examined, preferably for different batches of the material, as it might highly impact the results as shown in the following figure.

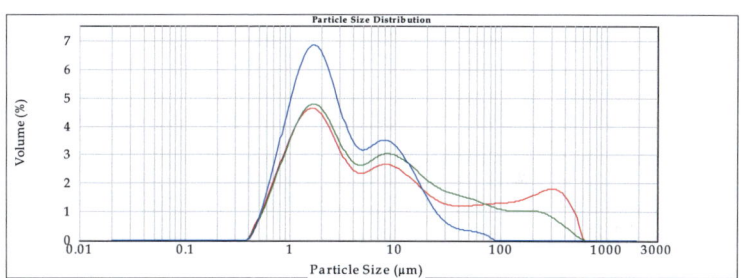

Red: No sonication, green: 10 seconds sonication, blue: 30 seconds sonication. Which is the more correct particle size distribution? It cannot be evaluated from this experiment – it can only be stated that the samples is very dependent on the degree of sonication! The results might imply that the sample is strongly aggregated – or that the particles are destroyed by sonication. An evaluation using a complementary method is required.

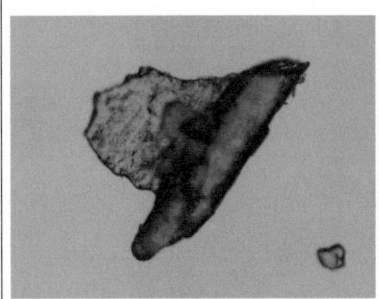 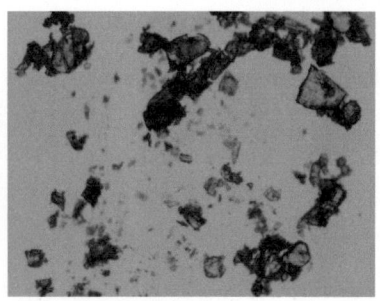

Particle before sonication: Some of the particles are observed as thin large flakes.

After sonication: The thin flakes have been broken down to much smaller particles. Thus sonication leads to strong alteration of the particles.

Pressure

For dry dispersion pressure is applied to the particles in order to obtain a uniform distribution in the laser beam. The degree of pressure used should be evaluated: As well as applying stirring and or sonication in wet dispersion, there is a risk that too high pressure alters the particle sizes. Part of the method validation is to expose the sample to various degrees of pressure in order to obtain a plateau where the particle size is constant. However, in practice a gradual decrease in particle size might be observed, thus the challenge is to find the optimal limit between breaking down particles and dispersing aggregates. Again, this implies that the results from the laser diffraction method should be compared to microscopy results after applying pressure.

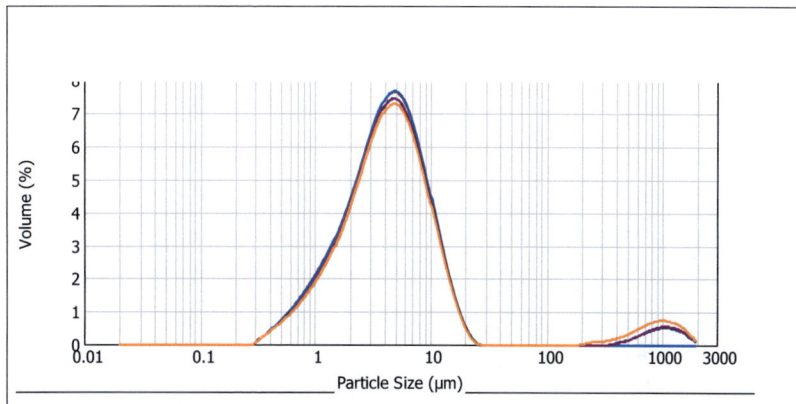

An example of results from laser diffraction measurements: A small peak with maximum around 1000 µm is observed. This peak might reflect:

1. *Large particles in the material (i.e. it actually reflects the particles in the material)*
2. *Aggregation of particles (i.e. it might be relevant to secure a better dispersion of particles by applying higher pressure)*

This can be evaluated by comparing to SEM results (to confirm/exclude presence of large particles) and by exposing the sample to various levels of pressure.

Number of sample preparations

The right the number of sample preparations should be chosen in order to get a statistically good description of the sizes.

According to Ph. Eur. 7.2 chapter 2.9.31 (Particle size analysis by laser light diffraction) it is stated that *"Mandatory limits cannot be specified in this monograph, as repeatabilities (different sample preparations) may vary appreciably from one substance to another. However, it is good practice to aim at acceptance criteria for repeatability such as $s_{rel} \leq 10$ per cent [n = 6] for any central value of the distribution (e.g. for x_{50}). Values at the sides of the distribution (e.g. x_{10} and x_{90}) are oriented towards less stringent acceptance criteria such as $s_{rel} \leq 15$ per cent [n = 6]. Below 10 µm, these values must be doubled"*. The symbol d is also widely used and the symbol x can thus be replaced by d.

Thus, in general one should aim for developing a method that gives results within these limits. However, in practice, the material might have special characteristics that leads to higher variations.

If the aim is to have, for instance, a RSD below 10%, the number of measurements needed for getting below this value can be determined experimentally for the material in question. In some cases, one determination might be sufficient to get a representative picture for the particle size distribution. However, in most cases you would use at least two sample preparations in order to verify the first result. Other samples might require more than two sample preparations – and in some cases, it might be unachievable to reach this RSD limit because of inherent properties of the material.

Reporting of results

Usually the particle size distribution will be reported as d(0.1), d(0.5) and d(0.9) – and as a *volume* size distribution. D10% - or d(0.1) - means that 10% of the particles (by volume) is below this size. It is also possible to report the sizes as a *number* distribution, but this is very seldom useful, as it is the amount – and not the number – of particles within a certain size range that is of interest (and by laser diffraction, it is the volume distribution that *is* measured). In the figure below an example of results from Mastersizer 2000 is seen and in the table next page the meaning of these parameters are described.

d(0.1): 3.848	d(0.5): 12.467	d(0.9): 63.607
Surface weighed mean: 5.960 µm	Vol. Weighed mean: 29.872 µm	
Meas. int.time: 3000 ms.	Obscuration: 15.55 %	Span: 4.794
Weighed residual: 0.342 %	Result unit: Volume	Result source: Average

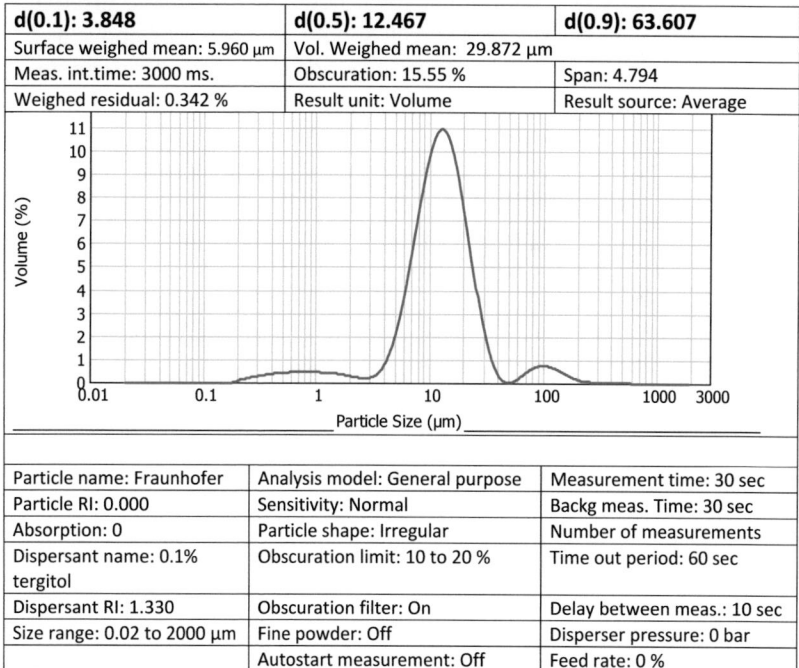

Particle name: Fraunhofer	Analysis model: General purpose	Measurement time: 30 sec
Particle RI: 0.000	Sensitivity: Normal	Backg meas. Time: 30 sec
Absorption: 0	Particle shape: Irregular	Number of measurements
Dispersant name: 0.1% tergitol	Obscuration limit: 10 to 20 %	Time out period: 60 sec
Dispersant RI: 1.330	Obscuration filter: On	Delay between meas.: 10 sec
Size range: 0.02 to 2000 µm	Fine powder: Off	Disperser pressure: 0 bar
	Autostart measurement: Off	Feed rate: 0 %

Example of a report template from Mastersizer 2000. In the current example it is shown for a wet dispersion method.

Parameter	Comments
Measurement integration time	Should be sufficiently long to assure a statistically good description of the size distribution. Limit is set during method development. This is the actual measuring time and for wet dispersion, this time should correspond to the time specified under "measurement time".
Obscuration	Shows the measured obscuration in the current measurement. Should be within the specified limits.
Span	Information about the width of the size distribution. In some cases relevant in QC.
Weighed residual	Information about how well the curve is fitted to the results. This should usually not be above a couple of percent – and even lower for a simple Gaussian distribution (i.e. higher for bimodal PSD).
Results unit	"Volume" (%) should always be used as laser diffraction measures volume size distribution. Translating these results into other parameters should be done with care!
Particle name	Fraunhofer or Mie. Fraunhofer often preferred for particles > 20 μm. Mie requires knowledge about RI and absorption of the material.
Particle RI	If Mie is used the value should be determined for the material in question
Absorption	If Mie is used the value should be determined for the material in question
Dispersant RI	The value for the given dispersion media should be used (these values are found in the literature for many solvents)
Particle shape	Particles are almost always "Irregular": Only for spherical reference materials it is changed (i.e. reference material).

Obscuration limit	Limits are set during method validation: Lower limit depends on signal to noise level. Higher limit is set to avoid multiple scattering
Obscuration filter	Should always be "on" in order to avoid measurement that are not within the above stated limits.
Measurement time	Should be sufficiently long to assure that all material is measured in the laser beam. This is especially important for dry dispersion. This time is set in the method: For wet dispersion, it should be sufficiently long to measure a representative amount of the particles in the sample. For dry dispersion, it should be sufficiently long to assure that the full sample amount has passed before the measurement has ended.
Disperser pressure	Used in dry dispersion measurements to secure optimal dispersion (i.e. dispersion without break-down of particles)
Feed rate	Used in dry dispersion measurements: Describes how fast the sample is disposed into the measuring area. Usually only informative: Can be adjusted to get within the specified obscuration limits. Informative: Used to control the obscuration. Should be set to allow a steady continuous flow of sample to achieve the desired obscuration.
Slit opening	Informative: Used to control the obscuration

Pitfalls in laser diffraction

As explained in the previous sections there are many parameters that should be taken into account when validating a laser diffraction method. Thus, in the performance of laser diffraction for determination of particle size distribution one should be aware of the many pitfalls. Some of these pitfalls are summarized in the following list:

-Sample **withdrawal** is not representative for the entire batch
-The sample **dissolves** in the dispersion.
-The sample **aggregates** in the dispersion media giving larger particle sizes than are the actual sizes in the product.
-If a part of the particles have high density, it is possible that **sedimentation** will occur, and thus, the whole sample will not be measured.
-**Creaming** is the case where a part of the sample floats on the dispersion media: The total amount of sample will not be measured - and the result will most likely not be representative for the product.

-**Sonication** is applied to disperse loose aggregates/agglomerates, but fragile primary particles are destroyed as well.
-**Air bubbles** in the system appears at the result as large particles
-A too high concentration (obscuration) causes **multiple scattering**. The background signal changes due to e.g. temperature changes. Variations in the background during measurement will influence the results.
-Wrong **values of refractive index** used (Mie theory) leading to misinterpretation of results particles.
-If the refractive index of the sample and of the dispersion media **is the same**, the laser beam cannot be diffracted.
-**Clear particles** reflects light, which is detected as small particles
-Due to the wavelength of the laser light, some **coloured samples** are not be measured.

When is your "validated method" valid?

Validation of a method for determination of particle sizes is based on the available batches at the time when the method is validated. Even though the validation is performed according to all current GMP rules one should always consider the risk if changes occur: All changes during manufacturing, i.e. change in equipment, processing parameters, solvents, etc. poses a risk that particle size and morphology changes. As laser diffraction is a robust method, most changes will be reflected in the results – but it has to be evaluated whether the changes observed actually corresponds to the particle changes (case 1).

Further, before starting up validation of a method, it should be evaluated what the purpose of the method is: Do you want to know the sizes of the primary particles – or are you interested in the sizes of the aggregates/agglomerates as they might largely affect the behaviour during processing? In the study presented in case 2, two batches of the same compound - from different suppliers and with quite different particle characteristics - were compared with regard to particle size and dissolution properties. One batch consisted of small -and agglomerated- particles and the others of larger particles that did not agglomerate. In contrast to "expected" behaviour, the smaller particles dissolved more slowly than the larger particles – probably because of their tendency to agglomerate. In this case, the size of the *primary* particles, as determined by the validated particle size method, does not give a good description of the product behaviour. Thus, the current example highlights the importance of correlating your method for determination of particle size to other critical parameters for the product in question.

In some cases, the same product actually requires two different methods: One for determination of aggregation, and one for determination of the size of the primary particles. Further, during validation the limitations of the method should be clear: Is the method valid if an overall change in morphology or size occur? Generally, this can only be verified experimentally, i.e. if changes in particle characteristics occur some degree of revalidation is required. Some examples are presented in the following pages.

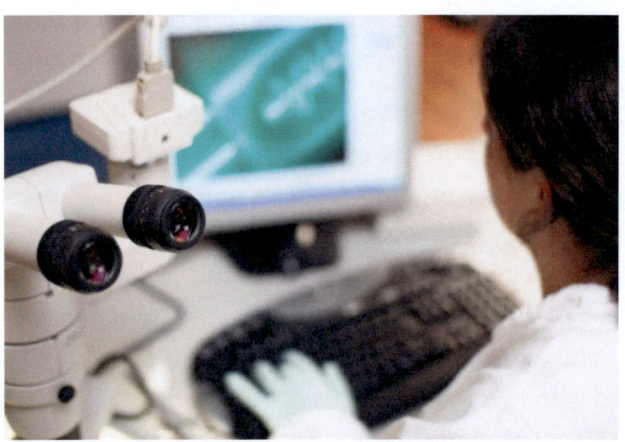

Case 1: Does the method apply to all batches?

A method for determination of particle sizes on a micronized material was developed. It was evaluated that wet dispersion in water was a suitable dispersion media, as no dissolution took place. However, it was further evaluated that sonication was necessary in order to avoid aggregation of these small particles during measurement. The method was fully validated without problems. However, later in development a new milling process was used. The laser diffraction results did not reveal major changes, so at first sight everything was OK. However, from microscopy it was discovered that the material actually did contain some large particles. It turned out that these large particles were broken down during sonication why they were not observed using laser diffraction. During revalidation of the method it was shown that even very slight stirring caused break-down of particles. Thus, a new dispersion media and minimal stirring was chosen.

Case 2: When particle size does not reflect product behaviour

When determining particle sizes by laser diffraction, the particles are always dispersed in a suitable medium (air or liquid). The dispersion medium - and mechanical conditions for the measurement (i.e. stirring/pressure) - is chosen in order to obtain the "optimal" dispersion of the particles – i.e. usually a dispersion of the primary particles. Thus, in many laser diffraction methods, the results reflect the size of the primary particles - and aggregates/agglomerates are not detected as they are dispersed by adding pressure, ultrasound or stirring. In the current example it is quite clear that the particle sizes measured by laser diffraction are the sizes of the primary particles. However, the size of the primary particles does not reflect the behaviour of the material:

One would normally assume that smaller particles would dissolve faster than the larger particles: It turns out not to be the case in the current example. The dissolution rate was measured for two batches of very different particle sizes. The results indicate that a slower dissolution takes place for the smaller particles – which probably reflect that large agglomerates contribute to slowing down the dissolution rate. Thus, in regard to evaluation of the dissolution rate a more fulfilling description would, in this case, have been obtained by "including" the size of the agglomerates in the laser diffraction measurement.

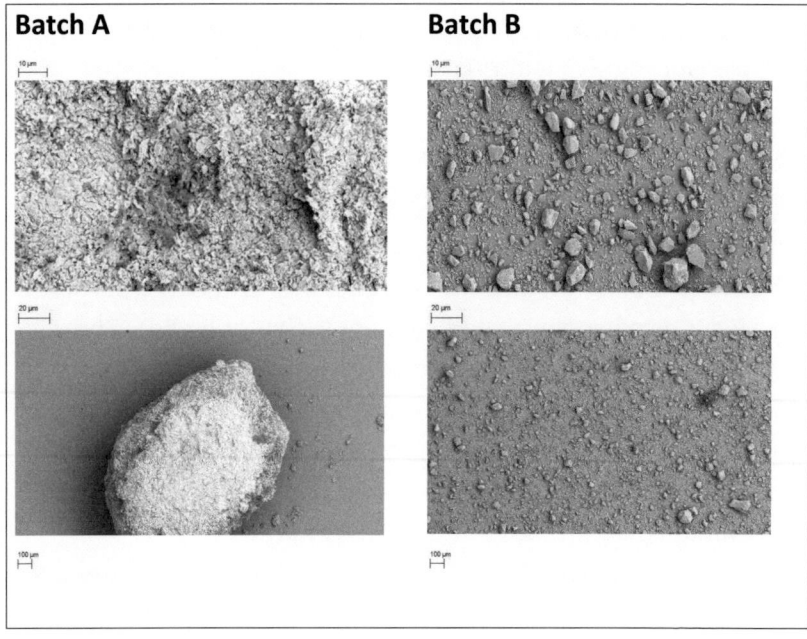

Batch A **Batch B**

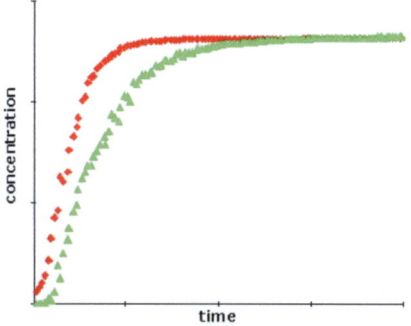

Dissolution rate of Batch A: Green and Batch B: Red

Two samples of compound X from different suppliers were examined by SEM (scanning electron microscopy), laser diffraction and dissolution. The chemical composition and the crystal form (as reflected by XRD) of the two batches are the same. Batch A consists of small primary particles building up large agglomerates. Batch B are made up of larger primary particles and does not agglomerate. The differences in particle size were further reflected in laser diffraction measurement: D90% is 19.7 μm for batch A and 51.9 μm for batch B. These results confirm that the primary particles of batch B are larger and those of batch A. However, the material composed of the larger particles dissolve faster than the small particles.

If you want to know the sizes of the primary particles, the method seems to be very reliable. However, because of the existence of large agglomerates in batch A it is quite likely that this batch would behave differently during processing than a product consisting of not-agglomerated particles of the same size. It might be relevant to test whether the agglomerates affect processability – and if they do (which is very likely) it might be a good idea to develop a laser diffraction method that does not lead to breakdown of the agglomerates.

These experiments illustrate the importance of correlating methods - and focusing on *the purpose* when developing a method for determination of particle sizes: Are you interested in the primary particles and/or the agglomerates? The tendency to agglomerate influences the dissolution rate – and it might further influence the manufacturing properties.

Thus, a method validation should include correlation of particle sizes to other parameters – such as for instance the dissolution rate, the water uptake or a specific processability parameter. In many cases it might actually be relevant to validate different particle size determination methods in order to be able to get a fulfilling description of the product in relation to different critical properties.

Revalidation required?

During validation of a method, a number of batches might be available – depending on the manufacturing process at the given time-point. Thus, the method is validated using specific batches – but depending on the robustness of the method, it might not be valid when receiving material from a new supplier.

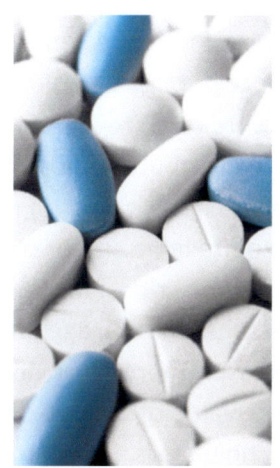

If the manufacturing process changes, or if you change supplier, you will always observe a change in the particle characteristics, either with regard to the size or the morphology of the particles. In these cases it should always be evaluated what impact these changes will have -not only on the particle size – but also on other critical parameters. Thus, you should reassure that the method you use for determination of particle sizes is still valid in order to describe the properties of your product correctly.

Summary and key learnings

- Particle size is by far the most important physical property of particulate samples in pharmaceutical development and has a direct influence on material properties such as processability and bioavailability for oral drugs.
- According to regulatory authorities (ICH guidelines), particle size distribution should be known – and controlled.
- Even slight changes in manufacturing conditions might lead to quite large size or morphology changes and these changes might be critical for the current product (blending properties, dissolution rate, agglomeration tendencies, etc.)
- Measurement of particle size is not an exact technique and a true value of the size does not exist. A range of analytical techniques is available for determination of particle size; these all have their strengths and weaknesses.
- Laser diffraction is the golden standard method for determination of particle sizes in the pharmaceutical industry using the other experimental methods in verification of the results.
- A thorough method development is always required when using laser diffraction in order to secure that the measurements actually reflect the particles in the sample.

10 tips for determination of particle sizes

1. Decide *the purpose* of the particle size determination: Do you want to know the size of the *primary* particles or are the sizes of agglomerates also important? The sizes of the agglomerates might be very relevant, for instance if you need information for optimizing processing conditions.

2. Decide whether **dry or wet dispersion** is the best method: Wet dispersion requires a smaller sample amount and is optimal for cohesive powders. Dry dispersion might be better suited if the powder is free flowing and/or contains large particles (400-600 mm).

3. For wet dispersion: **Test various dispersion media** and chose a medium where no dissolution takes place – and where the particle sizes are stable over time.

4. Test -and select- the **right sampling conditions** with regard to sonication and stirring speed (Again: Be aware of the purpose of the measurement).

5. Select the **right obscuration** interval: Too high obscuration leads to incorrect peaks – too low obscuration leads to imprecise measurements due to background noise.

6. For dry dispersion: **Choose a pressure** where the agglomerates are dispersed – but the primary particles remains intact.

7. Select the **correct calculation parameters** for "translating" the laser results into particle size: Choose either Mie or Fraunhofer. Mie might be a more correct model, but if Mie is used you have to *know* the refraction index of the particles – do not use assumptions, as this might lead to very strange results!

8. **Always use a complementary method** to verify your laser diffraction results. (Microscopy and SEM are very useful methods for this purpose).

9. Verify that the **mechanical treatment** (pressure, stirring, sonication) does not alter the particle size using a complementary method. Especially sonication might lead to quite drastic changes of the sizes.

10. Important: If processing conditions are changed – **always verify that the method still applies!** Even small changes in processing might lead to a quite significant change in size and morphology of the particles.

About Particle Analytical

Particle Analytical is a dynamic cGMP compliant company dedicated to supporting customers within the field of particle analysis/powder analysis. We focus first and foremost on the pharmaceutical industry and we support R&D, production and quality assurance. As one of the few companies in this field in Europe we offer full particle analysis/powder analysis – which includes particle size determination and examination of physical properties of particles.

Our analytical laboratory provides the pharmaceutical industry with physical-chemical development services. Our services include:

- Particle Size Determination
- Polymorph Screening/examination of crystalline structures
- Examination of Physical Properties (XRD, dissolution rate, water uptake, etc.)
- Method Development and Validation

Our services can either be used in routine analysis, separately to solve specific problems, or in parallel to a larger drug development program. Our aim is to be flexible and to understand our clients' requirements. If our expertise is required to tackle specific problems encountered during drug manufacture, Particle Analytical will provide an unrivalled service. Particle Analytical supports R&D, production and quality assurance.

Particle Analytical has all state of the art equipment for particle analysis. The instruments/methods are listed on the following page.